Spanish Speaking Countries

COLORING & HANDWRITING PRACTICE BOOK

SPAIN

spain

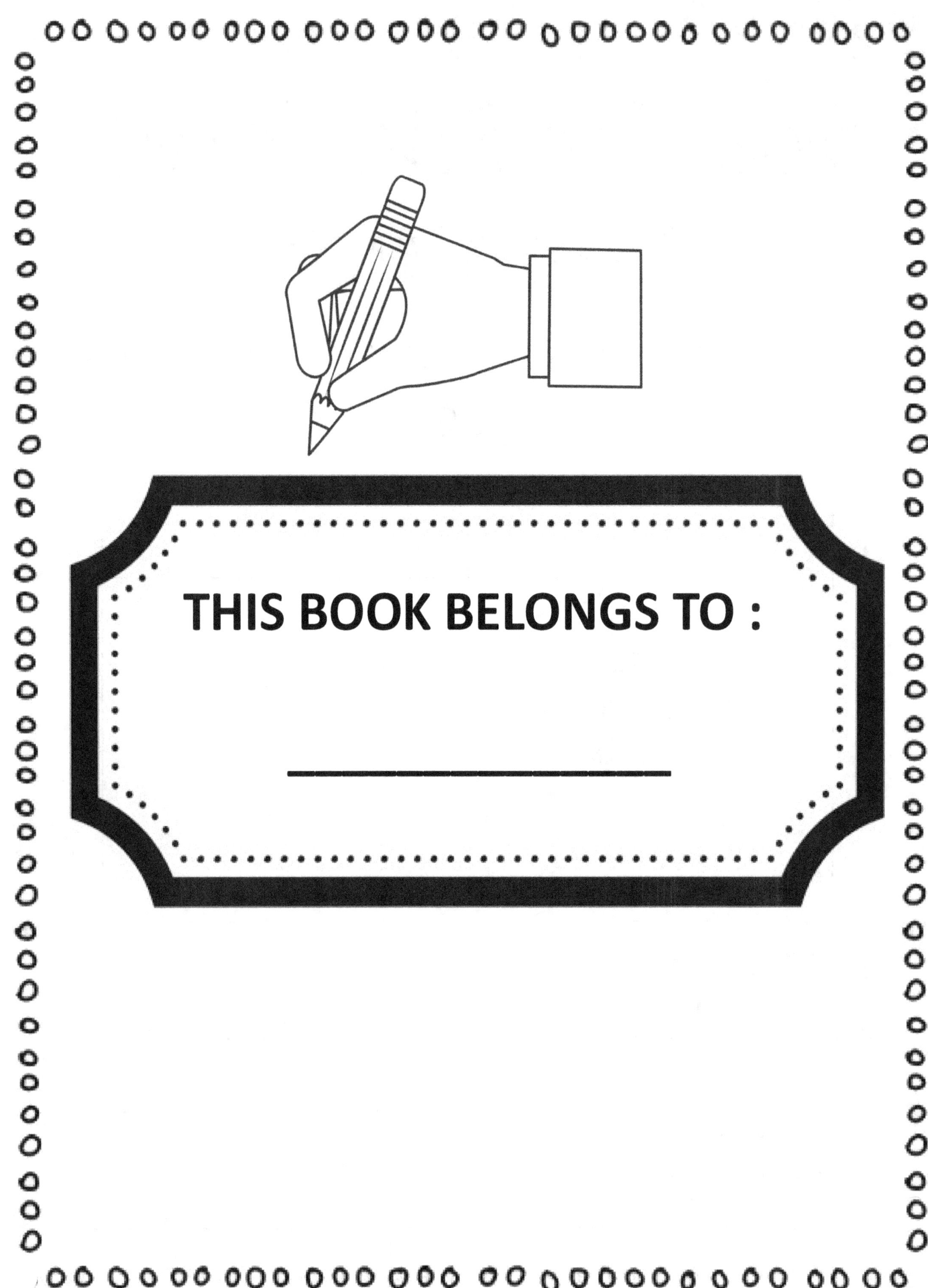

THIS BOOK BELONGS TO :

MEXICO

MEXICO

mexico

ARGENTINA

ARGENTINA

argentina

GUATEMALA

NAME : _________________________   DATE : _____________

GUATEMALA

guatemala

NAME : ___________________   DATE : ___________

COSTA RICA

COSTA RICA

costa rica

NAME : ___________________   DATE : ___________________

NICARAGUA

NICARAGUA

nicaragua

PANAMA

PANAMA

panama

HONDURAS

HONDURAS

honduras

NAME : ___________________   DATE : ___________

CUBA

CUBA

cuba

DOMINICAN REPUBLIC

DOMINICAN

republic

BOLIVIA

BOLIVIA

bolivia

NAME : ________________   DATE : ____________

PARAGUAY

PAGARUAY

paraguay

NAME : ___________________   DATE : ____________

CHILE

CHILE

chile

NAME : _________________________   DATE : _____________

COLOMBIA

COLOMBIA

colombia

EL SALVADOR

EL SALVADOR

el salvador

NAME : ________________   DATE : ____________

URUGUAY

URUGUAY

uruguay

NAME : ______________________   DATE : __________

ECUADOR

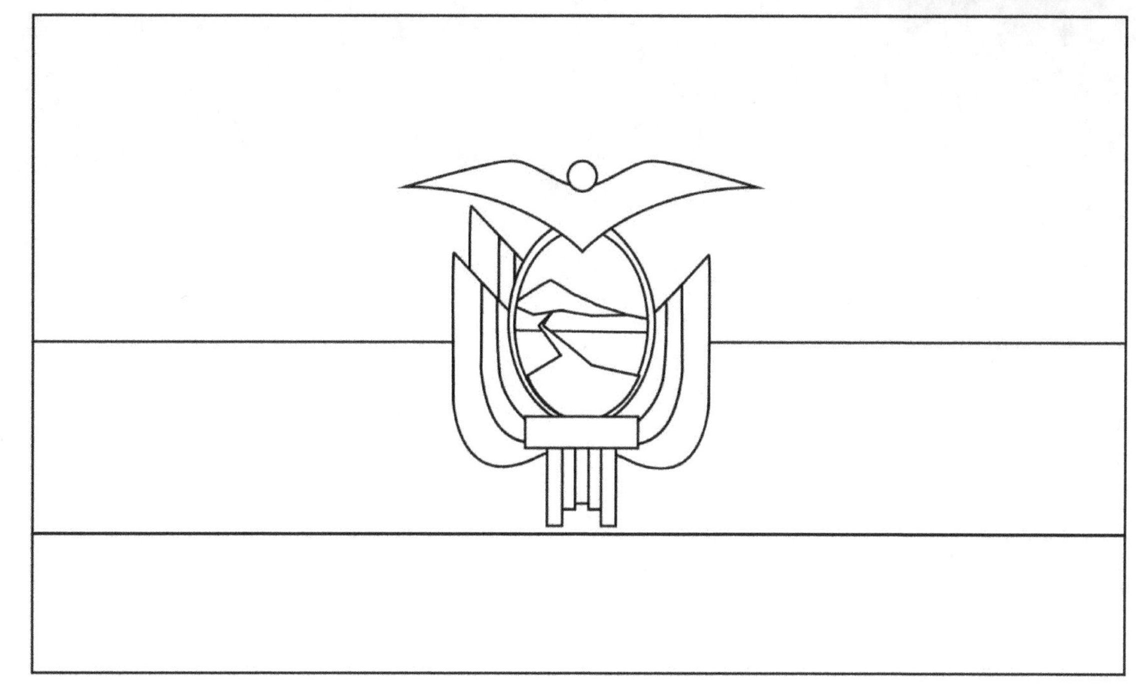

ECUADOR

ecuador

NAME : ___________________   DATE : ____________

PERU

PERU

peru

VENEZUELA

VENEZUELA

venezuela

PUERTO RICO

NAME : _______________   DATE : _______________

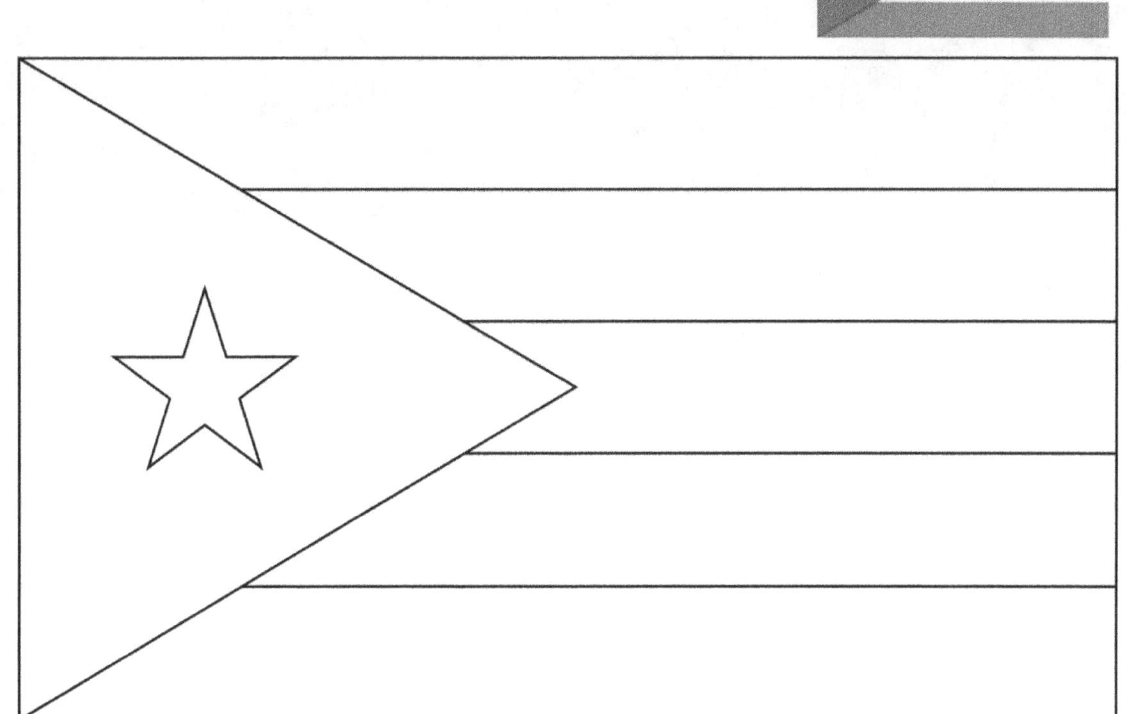

PUERTO RICO

puerto rico

EQUATORIAL GUINEA

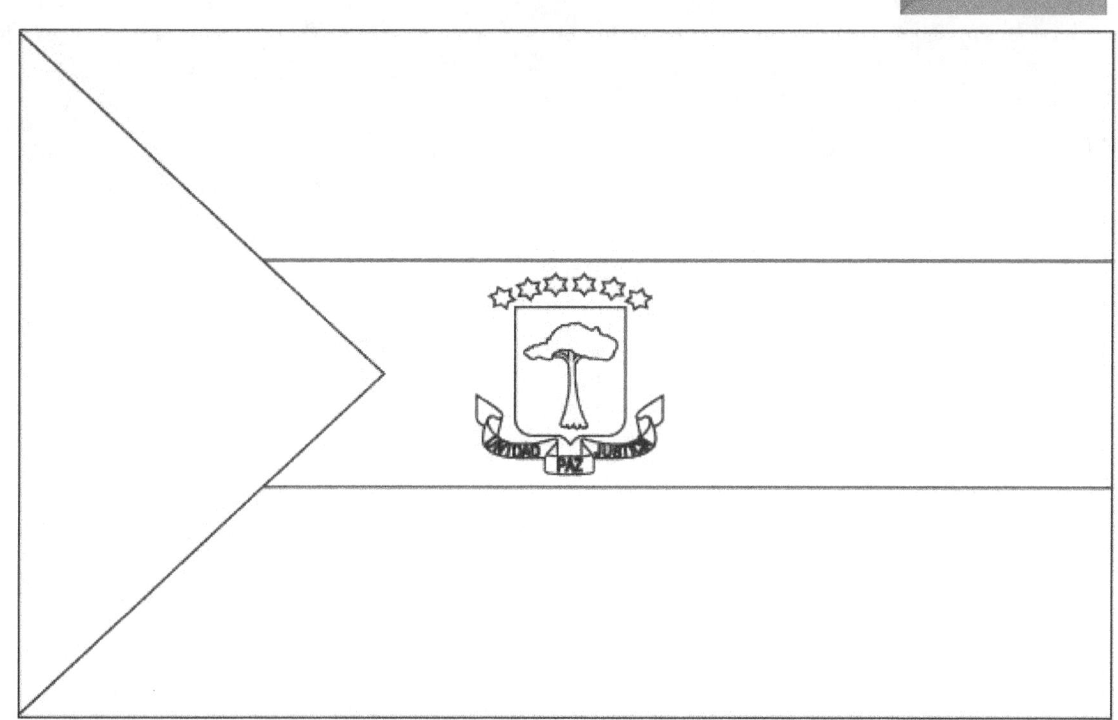

EQUATORIAL

guinea

www.ingramcontent.com/pod-product-compliance
Lightning Source LLC
Chambersburg PA
CBHW081827250726
48657CB00011B/3508